FREEDOM'S PROMISE

THE 1924 IMMIGRATION ACT
AND ITS RELEVANCE TODAY

BY DUCHESS HARRIS, JD, PHD
WITH CAROLYN WILLIAMS-NOREN

Core Library

An Imprint of Abdo Publishing
abdobooks.com

Cover image: Immigrants wait in line to leave Ellis
Island in the early 1900s.

abdobooks.com

Published by Abdo Publishing, a division of ABDO, PO Box 398166, Minneapolis, Minnesota 55439. Copyright © 2020 by Abdo Consulting Group, Inc. International copyrights reserved in all countries. No part of this book may be reproduced in any form without written permission from the publisher. Core Library™ is a trademark and logo of Abdo Publishing.

Printed in the United States of America, North Mankato, Minnesota
092019
012020

THIS BOOK CONTAINS
RECYCLED MATERIALS

Cover Photo: Bettmann/Getty Images
Interior Photos: Bettmann/Getty Images, 1; Everett Historical/Shutterstock Images, 5, 19; The Print Collector Heritage Images/Newscom, 6–7, 43; AP Images, 8, 31; Detroit Publishing Company/Glasshouse Images/Newscom, 11; Andre Jenny Stock Connection Worldwide/ Newscom, 14–15; North Wind Picture Archives, 16; National Park Service/Statue of Liberty National Monument/AP Images, 24–25; Red Line Editorial, 26, 37; Yoichi Okam/LBJ Library/CNP/Newscom, 32; Kit Leong/Shutterstock Images, 34–35

Editor: Maddie Spalding
Series Designer: Ryan Gale

Library of Congress Control Number: 2019942002

Publisher's Cataloging-in-Publication Data

Names: Harris, Duchess, author. | Williams-Noren, Carolyn, author.
Title: The 1924 immigration act and its relevance today / by Duchess Harris and Carolyn Williams-Noren
Description: Minneapolis, Minnesota : Abdo Publishing, 2020 | Series: Freedom's promise | Includes online resources and index.
Identifiers: ISBN 9781532190889 (lib. bdg.) | ISBN 9781532176739 (ebook)
Subjects: LCSH: Immigrants--Legal status, laws, etc--Juvenile literature. | United States-- Emigration and immigration--History--20th century--Juvenile literature. | Immigrants-- United States--History--19th century--Juvenile literature. | Race discrimination-- Juvenile literature. | Citizenship--United States--History. | Xenophobia--Juvenile literature.
Classification: DDC 325.252--dc23

CONTENTS

A LETTER FROM DUCHESS

Students don't always realize how much teachers learn from teaching. I am a college professor, and I learned a lot when we discussed the 1924 Immigration Act in class. I read about a man named Takao Ozawa.

Mr. Ozawa was born in Japan in 1875. He immigrated to San Francisco, California, in 1894. He graduated high school in California. He later moved to Hawaii. Ozawa wanted to become a US citizen, but the Supreme Court rejected his request in 1922. The court said only white people could be citizens. It concluded that Japanese people could not be white. This court ruling set the stage for the Immigration Act of 1924. This act prevented people from Asia from coming to the United States. It also set limits on immigration from certain parts of Europe.

Today, immigration is often in the news. It is not a new topic. America has a long history of deciding who is allowed citizenship and who isn't. Please join me on a journey that explores who has the freedom to call the United States their country and who is denied this promise.

Duchess Harris

Italian immigrants wait to be processed at Ellis Island in the early 1900s.

A NEW ACT

Senator Ellison D. Smith of South Carolina stood on the floor of the US Senate. The date was April 9, 1924. The Senate was debating a bill about immigration. The bill would restrict the number of immigrants allowed into the United States. Smith supported the bill. He urged other senators to do the same. He said the country should "shut the door" on immigrants.

Immigrants are people who settle in a new country. In the late 1800s and early 1900s, approximately 14 percent of Americans were immigrants. The Immigration Act would limit the number of immigrants allowed from each country. The limits were

Immigrants came to the United States on ships. Large ships could hold up to 2,000 people.

7

Smith, *left*, served as a US senator from 1909 to 1944.

called quotas. The act would let many people from northern and western Europe immigrate to the United States. But it would reduce the number of immigrants from southern and eastern Europe. The act would ban all Asian immigrants.

SMITH'S BELIEFS

Smith and some other politicians thought the United States was becoming overcrowded. In his speech before the Senate, Smith said immigrants would use up the country's resources. He feared that people would start to fight over land.

Smith believed people from some countries had more desirable traits than people from other countries. He favored northern European immigrants. Many other Americans shared this belief. The United States has a democratic government. In a democracy, the public has a say in how the government is run. In the 1920s, many other parts of the world did not have democracies. Smith thought people from those areas

"SCIENTIFIC" RACISM

In the 1920s, many white Americans held racist beliefs. They thought northern Europeans were naturally smart, healthy, wealthy, and honest. They thought people from other parts of Europe were inferior. They also thought this of Native Americans, Asians, and Africans. Racist white Americans believed parents passed down inferior qualities to their children. They used scientific words such as "data" and "traits" to talk about their beliefs. Science and history have proved these ideas wrong. They are untrue, unfair, and harmful. But these beliefs were popular in the early 1900s. They help explain why many Americans supported the Immigration Act.

needed a ruler to tell them what to do. He did not think they would be able to participate in a democracy. Because of this, he wanted to stop or slow immigration from certain countries. These countries included Italy and Poland. They also included Asian countries.

In Smith's speech, he repeated "shut the door" several times. He was referring to Ellis Island. Many immigrants came to the country through this station. Ellis Island was in New York Harbor. Many people called it the "golden door" to the United States. It was the main station for immigrants from southern and eastern Europe. The station's peak years of operation were from 1900 to 1914. In those years, approximately 5,000 to 10,000 people arrived at the station each day.

FIGHTING THE BILL

One person who disagreed with Smith was Robert H. Clancy. Clancy was a congressman. He spoke out against the Immigration Act. He said the bill treated

In the early 1900s, the Lower East Side in New York City was the largest Jewish neighborhood in the United States.

people unfairly based on where they came from. This was a form of racial discrimination.

Clancy described the immigrants in his home city of Detroit, Michigan. Some were from Poland or Italy. Others were Jewish people from eastern Europe. Clancy said these immigrants worked hard and supported the country.

Clancy also talked about his own ancestors' immigration. He argued that immigration is an important part of American history. He said the Immigration Act was un-American.

PERSPECTIVES

A LETTER OF PROTEST

Some people opposed the Immigration Act. Recent immigrants spoke out against the act. Members of the Croatian League of Illinois wrote a letter to their representatives in Congress. They hoped the bill would not pass. In the letter, they described their loyalty to the United States during World War I (1914–1918). They said they were "useful citizens." They explained that Croatian and Yugoslavian immigrants had "done much to build up the wealth and prosperity of the country."

Most Congress members voted to pass the Immigration Act. The House of Representatives passed it with a vote of 322 to 71. In the Senate, it passed with a vote of 62 to 6. On May 26, 1924, President Calvin Coolidge signed the bill into law.

The Immigration Act of 1924 is sometimes called the Johnson-Reed Act. This name comes from two congressmen who supported it. One was Representative Albert Johnson. The other was Senator David A. Reed. Both were members of the Republican Party.

Immigration was a major topic of conversation in the 1920s. Americans debated whether immigration helped or harmed the United States. They argued about how many immigrants the country could hold. The Immigration Act created greater immigration restrictions. These restrictions were in place for more than 40 years. In some ways, the Immigration Act still shapes how the United States handles immigration today.

EXPLORE ONLINE

Chapter One talks about Ellis Island. The article at the website below goes into more depth on this topic. As you know, every source is different. How is the information from the website the same as the information in Chapter One? What new facts did you learn?

INTERACTIVE TOUR OF ELLIS ISLAND
abdocorelibrary.com/1924-immigration-act

EARLY IMMIGRATION

mmigrants have been settling in the United States for hundreds of years. The first Spanish and French immigrants came to the present-day United States in the 1500s. In the 1600s, the first English immigrants arrived. They settled along the East Coast. They created colonies on lands where Native peoples had lived for thousands of years.

In 1607, approximately 100 English immigrants arrived in the present-day United States. They formed the first English colony in North America. They called their colony Jamestown, Virginia. More immigrants came

A sculpture in Albuquerque, New Mexico, depicts Spanish settlers who explored the present-day United States.

The English immigrants who built the Jamestown colony sailed across the Atlantic Ocean in three ships.

to North America in the following years. Another group of English settlers landed in present-day Cape Cod, Massachusetts, in 1620. Many of them came to North America to escape discrimination. People in England discriminated against them because of their religion. They formed a colony they called Plymouth.

English immigrants formed 13 colonies along the East Coast. By 1770 more than 2 million people lived in these colonies. Some of them were enslaved Africans. The English had brought them to the colonies on ships starting in 1619.

In 1776 the colonists declared their independence from England. They formed a new nation. They called it the United States of America.

SOURCES OF IMMIGRANTS

The number of immigrants in the United States grew steadily from 1840 through the early 1920s. Before 1890 most immigrants came from northern and western Europe. Many came from Germany, Ireland, England, Sweden, and Norway. Most were Protestant Christians. Many white Americans were also Protestants. They saw these immigrants as similar to themselves. For this reason, some people welcomed these immigrants. Still, anti-immigrant attitudes took root. Many Irish immigrants were Catholic. Protestants often disliked Catholics. Some attacked Irish immigrants' homes.

Another large immigrant group in the mid-1800s was Asian immigrants. These people came to the United States from China, Japan, and other Asian countries. They sought better jobs and opportunities. But they faced widespread discrimination. Asian immigrants were not allowed to become US citizens.

In the 1890s, the number of immigrants from northern and western Europe declined. More immigrants came from southern and eastern Europe. People came from Italy, Austria-Hungary, Russia, and Poland. Many of these immigrants were Catholic or Jewish. Many white Americans saw these immigrants as very different from themselves. Some Americans called them the "new" immigrants.

OPINIONS ON IMMIGRATION

In the late 1800s, "scientific" racist ideas were widely taken as truth. Books argued that people from northern

Many Chinese immigrants formed their own communities, called Chinatowns, in the United States.

Europe had the most desirable traits. Many Americans wanted to slow or stop immigration. They wanted to keep out the people they thought were inferior. These people included the "new" immigrants.

Not all Americans held these beliefs. But some supported immigration restrictions for other reasons. For example, African Americans were just beginning to find good job opportunities in northern cities. Many of them feared losing their jobs to immigrants. For that reason, some wanted to slow or stop immigration.

Other Americans supported immigration. Many people in northern cities welcomed immigrants. These cities relied on immigrant workers.

IMMIGRATION LAWS

In the late 1800s and early 1900s, Congress passed many immigration laws. These laws limited the number of immigrants allowed into the country. Many laws reduced the number of Asian immigrants. The first of these was the Chinese Exclusion Act of 1882. This act said Chinese workers could not come into the country. It also prevented Chinese immigrants from becoming US citizens.

During World War I (1914–1918), many people fled the fighting in Europe. They tried to immigrate to the United States. Many Americans opposed this increased immigration. In response, Congress passed the Immigration Act of 1917. This act kept out people with certain diseases and disabilities. The act also required all immigrant adults to take a reading test. They could take the test in their native language. Adults who could not read were not allowed into the country.

The Immigration Act of 1917 also created an "Asiatic Barred Zone." This region included much of eastern Asia and the Pacific Islands. People from these places were not allowed to come to the United States.

THE US CENSUS

A census is an official count of a country's population. The US census happens every ten years. It usually asks about each person's name, age, job, and birthplace. The government uses the census results to decide how to spend money. The results also determine how many representatives each state has in Congress.

In 1921 the Emergency Quota Act passed. It paved the way for the 1924 Immigration Act. The 1921 law created quotas. It only allowed 350,000 immigrants into the United States each year. Each country's quota was based on the 1910 US census. The census is a population count. The 1910 census showed how many immigrants from each country were in the United States. Immigration from each country was limited to 3 percent of that number per year. Within a few years, the Immigration Act of 1924 would create further restrictions.

STRAIGHT TO THE
SOURCE

Frederic C. Howe was an immigration official in the early 1900s. He helped process immigrants at Ellis Island. He wrote:

As an immigration official I presided over Ellis Island for five years. During this time probably a million immigrants arrived at the port of New York. They were for the most part poor. They had that in common with the early immigrant. They had other qualities in common. They were ambitious and filled with hope. They were for the most part kindly and moved by the same . . . virtues as other peoples. . . . It was not political liberty, religious liberty, or personal liberty that changed the early immigrant of Northern Europe into the American of today. His qualities were born of . . . equal opportunity with his fellows to make his life what he would have it to be.

Source: Frederic C. Howe. "The Alien." *Civilization in the United States: An Inquiry by Thirty Americans*. Ed. Harold E. Stearns. Rahway, New Jersey: Harcourt, 1922. Print. 341.

What's the Big Idea?

Take a close look at this passage. Howe met many immigrants when he worked on Ellis Island. What main point is he making here about how immigrants should be treated?

GREATER RESTRICTIONS

The 1924 Immigration Act was the most restrictive immigration law to date. Like the 1921 Emergency Quota Act, it included quotas for each country. But it changed the way the quotas were set. The 1924 act still based each country's quota on the US census. But it did not use a recent census. It used the 1890 census. In 1890 the number of Americans who had come from southern and eastern Europe was low. As a result, the act cut off nearly all newcomers from those regions.

The 1924 law considered the national origins of all citizens. Many citizens had

Many immigrants from Austria-Hungary left their homeland to escape poverty.

QUOTAS

COUNTRY	QUOTA
Germany	51,227
Great Britain and Northern Ireland	34,007
Poland	5,982
Russia	2,248
Hungary	473
Egypt	100

This chart shows the quotas set for certain countries by the 1924 Immigration Act. Which countries were allowed the largest numbers of immigrants? Which were allowed very few? How did racism influence these decisions?

northern European origins. For this reason, many of the immigrants allowed in each year would come from northern Europe. The law also shrank each country's quota to 2 percent. The minimum quota per country was 100 people. In total, only 165,000 immigrants were allowed into the United States each year.

EFFECTS

The Immigration Act kept out anyone who could not become a US citizen. Asian immigrants could not become citizens. So they could no longer come to the United States. Before the Immigration Act, the United States and Japan had an agreement. Japanese workers had been allowed into the country. The Immigration Act ended this agreement.

The Immigration Act favored certain immigrant groups over others. People of Mexican, Canadian, and South American descent lived in the United States in 1890. But the Immigration Act did not limit immigration from those countries.

The law also did not apply the quota rule equally. For example, officials did not count Americans of African descent when creating the quotas. Only 100 people from each African country were allowed into the United States each year. White people who lived in African countries filled most of these slots.

THE *ST. LOUIS*

For some people, the quotas were a matter of life or death. The total immigrant quota was reduced to 153,879 in 1929. The quotas for eastern and southern European countries dropped. This included the countries of Germany, Poland, and Romania. Many Jewish people lived in these countries. They were persecuted in the 1930s. At that time, the Nazi Party ruled Germany. The Nazis invaded neighboring countries. They imprisoned and killed Jewish people. This genocide was called the Holocaust.

In 1939 a group of 937 people left Germany. Most were Jewish. They sailed across the Atlantic Ocean in a ship called the *St. Louis*. They tried to enter Cuba, but Cuban officials would not accept them. The ship headed toward Florida. But the US government also did not allow the ship to dock. The Jewish people were refugees, not immigrants. Refugees are forced to leave their homes because of violence or persecution. But the government considered them immigrants. Officials did not want to go over the immigration quotas.

CHANGING RELATIONSHIPS

The 1924 Immigration Act shaped the course of US history. For example, it changed the relationship between the United States and Japan. The two countries had been friendly with each other. But many Japanese people were angered when the United States ended its immigration agreement. Some historians see this as a turning point. They say it set the countries on the path to becoming enemies during World War II (1939–1945).

The *St. Louis* had to sail back to Europe after Canada also refused them. Some European countries accepted the refugees.

The Nazis captured and killed some of these people. Of the 937 refugees, the Nazis killed 254. During the Holocaust, the Nazis and their supporters murdered approximately 6 million Jewish people. More of these people might have found safety in the United States if US immigration laws had been different.

THE END OF THE ACT

The Immigration Act's quotas were in place for nearly 40 years. During those years, Congress made a few changes to US immigration law. A 1948 law loosened the quotas to let in refugees after World War II (1939–1945). In 1952 the McCarran-Walter Act passed. It ended the ban on Asian immigrants. Then in the mid-1950s, the United States let in 38,000 refugees from Hungary. These refugees had been persecuted in their home country.

In 1965 a new law replaced the Immigration Act. It was called the Immigration and Naturalization Act, or

Cuban officials turned away the *St. Louis* because they said its passengers did not meet the requirements to enter the country.

President Lyndon B. Johnson signed the Hart-Celler Act into law on October 3, 1965.

the Hart-Celler Act. This law still limited the total number of immigrants each year. But it ended the national origin quotas. One of the law's goals was to reunite immigrant families. The law also let in well-educated immigrants or immigrants who had special job skills.

STRAIGHT TO THE
SOURCE

Morris Abraham Schneider was a Polish immigrant who came to the United States in 1920. He was 10 years old at the time. He later described his journey:

I [had never been] on a ship before and . . . I was awed by it. It was overwhelming. All the people and boarding the ship, it was all a brand new experience. . . .

Steerage was one huge place. It was the lowest deck. . . . It was very hot, compounded by the fact that there must have been anywhere from two to three hundred people in that huge cavernous area. The body smells, the body odors, the lack of sanitation, the lack of any kind of facilities, washing, there was no such thing as washing or bathing. The stench, the vermin, it was rat infested.

Source: Ellis Island Oral History Collection. "Morris Remembers the Steamship (Transcript)." Interviewed by Paul E. Sigrist Jr. *National Park Service*. National Park Service, November 17, 1991. Web. Accessed July 22, 2019.

Consider Your Audience

Adapt this passage for a different audience, such as your friends. Write a blog post conveying this same information for the new audience. How does your post differ from the original text and why?

LEGACY

Today, immigrants to the United States come from many countries. People from Mexico and South and Central America are the largest immigrant groups. Immigration from Asia and Africa is also increasing. In 2017 immigrants made up 13.7 percent of the US population. That was the highest percentage since 1910. Researchers predict that this number will keep growing.

The Immigration Act of 1924 is widely seen as racist today. Still, the laws of the 1920s influenced modern immigration laws. Current immigration debates also have similarities to debates that happened nearly 100 years ago.

Chinese Americans celebrate their heritage through parades and other events.

LEGAL IMMIGRATION

Illegal immigration is often in the news. But most immigrants are in the United States legally. In 2017, 77 percent of immigrants entered the country legally. Only 23 percent arrived illegally. A 2018 poll found that most Americans were not aware of this fact. Only 45 percent of respondents knew that most US immigration is legal. Thirty-five percent thought most immigrants entered illegally. Thirteen percent were unsure. Six percent thought there were equal numbers of illegal and legal immigrants.

Entering a country without permission is called *illegal immigration*. In 2016 Donald Trump was elected US president. He focused on illegal immigration. He thought too many people entered the country illegally. Trump and his supporters chanted "build the wall" to express their desire to end illegal immigration. In 1924 Smith's call to "shut the door" was not about a real door. But "build the wall" was a call for a physical wall along the US-Mexico border.

IMMIGRATION SINCE
1920

This graph shows how the makeup of immigrants in the United States has changed from 1920 to 2017. It shows immigrants as the percentage of the US population in these years. How have these numbers changed over time? How did the 1924 Immigration Act affect these numbers?

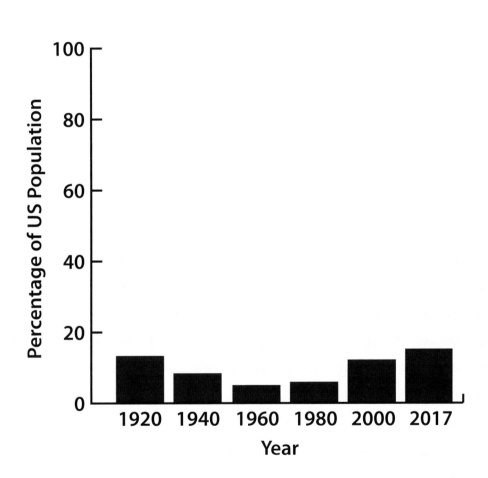

LIMITS ON IMMIGRATION

Current US laws still place limits on immigration.
To immigrate, a person must have a special document.
This document is called a visa. People who have a
parent, child, or spouse who is a US citizen are allowed
to immigrate. They can get a family visa. There is
no limit on the number of family visas. But many
immigrants do not meet these requirements. Only
226,000 visas are available for these people each year.
Up to 140,000 more visas can go to people with special
job skills. People who do not fit in these categories can
enter a drawing called a lottery. But not all countries
qualify for this lottery. People from some countries
cannot enter. Those who are chosen can get a visa. The
government gives up to 50,000 lottery visas each year.

Today, many Americans are divided on immigration.
Some think more immigrants should be allowed into
the country. Others think immigration should be more
restricted. In May 2019, Trump proposed changes to
the US immigration system. The changes would make it

more difficult for some people to get visas. Family visas would only be for spouses and children of authorized US residents. Trump also talked about a points system. It would give immigrants points for being young and wealthy. It would also give points for having valuable skills and advanced degrees. The visas would only go to those with the most points. The plan would get rid of the lottery system. It would require all immigrants

PERSPECTIVES
JEFF SESSIONS

Jeff Sessions has served as a senator and as the US attorney general. As attorney general, he had the power to shape US policies. Sessions was against immigration. In a 2015 interview, he praised the 1924 Immigration Act. He talked about the high percentage of immigrants. He said, "When the numbers reached about this high in 1924, the president and congress changed the policy. . . . It was good for America." He faced backlash after making this comment. Many people pointed out that the Immigration Act was discriminatory.

to learn English. They would also have to pass a test about the US government.

VIEWS ON IMMIGRANTS

In 1924 most Americans thought national origin quotas were a good idea. Some people have similar views today. In 2018 Trump spoke positively about immigrants from Norway. But he publicly wondered why the United States would want immigrants from Haiti. He also insulted immigrants from African countries.

Trump also discriminated against Muslims. He blamed Muslims for violent crimes. He said Muslims should not be allowed to enter the United States. In his first weeks as president, Trump temporarily banned travel to the United States from seven countries. The countries were all Muslim-majority countries.

Some people supported the president's order. But protests against it were widespread. The Muslim ban was challenged in court several times. Trump proposed several versions of the ban. In June 2018, the Supreme

Court approved a version of the ban. This version did not only include Muslim-majority countries. It also banned travel from Venezuela and North Korea.

LOOKING AHEAD

The Immigration Act was one way the United States handled immigration in the past. Its legacy is still visible today. It has influenced the way Americans think and talk about immigration. Learning this history can help people better understand immigration laws today.

FURTHER EVIDENCE

Chapter Four describes immigration to the United States today. What was one of the main points of this chapter? What key evidence supports this point? The website below features interviews with immigrants from different countries. Does the information on the website support the point you identified? Does it present new evidence?

INTERVIEWS WITH TODAY'S IMMIGRANTS
abdocorelibrary.com/1924-immigration-act

FAST FACTS

- Before 1890 most US immigrants came from northern and western Europe.

- From 1890 to 1924, most US immigrants came from southern and eastern Europe.

- The 1924 Immigration Act restricted immigration to the United States. It set a limit of 165,000 immigrants each year. It set different quotas for each country. The quotas let in more immigrants from northern and western Europe but reduced the number of immigrants from other countries. The act banned all immigration from Asia.

- The Immigration Act is widely recognized as discriminatory because it was based on racist ideas about who belonged in the United States.

- The Hart-Celler Act was passed in 1965. It ended the national origin quotas.

- In 2017 immigrants made up 13.7 percent of the US population.

- Modern ideas about legal and illegal immigration can be traced back to the immigration laws of the 1920s. The idea of a quota system also came from these laws.

STOP AND
THINK

Why Do I Care?

The Immigration Act of 1924 was overturned more than 50 years ago. But that doesn't mean you can't think about its influence today. How might your life or the lives of others be different if the Immigration Act had not been passed?

Take a Stand

Imagine you are a lawmaker today. Your job is to make new immigration laws. What factors do you need to consider when writing these laws? How could you try to make immigration laws fair to everyone?

Dig Deeper

After reading this book, what questions do you still have about the 1924 Immigration Act? With an adult's help, find a few reliable sources that can help answer your questions. Write a paragraph about what you learned.

GLOSSARY

colonies
lands owned by a faraway country or nation

discrimination
the unjust treatment of a group of people based on their race, gender, or other characteristics

genocide
the mass murder of people who belong to a certain group and the destruction of their culture

immigrants
people who leave their homelands to settle in another country

inferior
considered to be of lesser quality

origin
the beginning or source of something

persecute
to treat people cruelly because of their race or other characteristics

quota
a fixed number that is used to meet a requirement

racism
the belief that one race is superior to all others

refugees
people who have to leave their home country because of war or other disasters

ONLINE
RESOURCES

To learn more about the 1924 Immigration Act, visit our free resource websites below.

Visit **abdocorelibrary.com** or scan this QR code for free Common Core resources for teachers and students, including vetted activities, multimedia, and booklinks, for deeper subject comprehension.

Visit **abdobooklinks.com** or scan this QR code for free additional online weblinks for further learning. These links are routinely monitored and updated to provide the most current information available.

LEARN
MORE

Flatt, Lizann. *Immigration*. New York: Crabtree Publishing Company, 2015.

Otfinoski, Steven. *Immigration & America*. New York: Scholastic, 2018.

ABOUT THE
AUTHORS

Duchess Harris, JD, PhD

Dr. Harris is a professor of American Studies at Macalester College and curator of the Duchess Harris Collection of ABDO books. She is also the coauthor of the titles in the collection, which features popular selections such as *Hidden Human Computers: The Black Women of NASA* and series including News Literacy and Being Female in America.

Before working with ABDO, Dr. Harris authored several other books on the topics of race, culture, and American history. She served as an associate editor for *Litigation News*, the American Bar Association Section of Litigation's quarterly flagship publication, and was the first editor in chief of *Law Raza*, an interactive online journal covering race and the law, published at William Mitchell College of Law. She has earned a PhD in American Studies from the University of Minnesota and a JD from William Mitchell College of Law.

Carolyn Williams-Noren

Carolyn Williams-Noren writes poems, essays, and nonfiction books for young people. Some of her ancestors were immigrants, and so are some of her neighbors. She lives in Minneapolis with her husband and two daughters.

INDEX